D0873896

WITHDRAWN
No longer the property of the
Boston Public Library.
Sale of this material benefits the Library.

XTREME PETS
REPTILES

BY S.L. HAMILTON

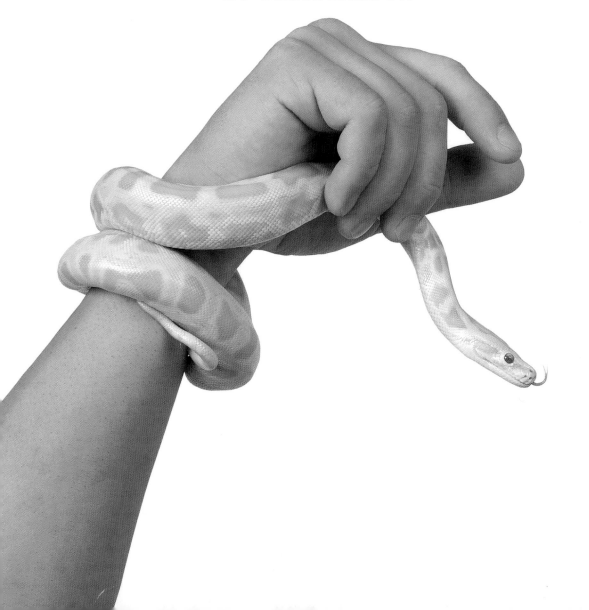

Visit us at
www.abdopublishing.com

Printed in the United States of America, North Mankato, Minnesota.
032013
092013

 PRINTED ON RECYCLED PAPER

Editor: John Hamilton
Graphic Design: Sue Hamilton
Cover Design: Sue Hamilton
Cover Photo: Getty Images
Interior Photos: AP-pgs 4-5, 14-15; Corbis-pg-28; Dreamstime-pgs 12-13, 16-17, 18 (inset), 26-27 & 29; Getty Images-pgs 9 & 10-11; Glow Images-pg 8; iStockphoto-pgs 18-19; Thinkstock-pgs 1, 2-3, 6-7, 20-21, 22-23, 24-25, 30-31 & 32.

ABDO Booklinks
Web sites about Xtreme Pets are featured on our Book Links pages. These links are routinely monitored and updated to provide the most current information available.
Web site: www.abdopublishing.com

Library of Congress Control Number: 2013931676

Cataloging-in-Publication Data

Hamilton, Sue.
 Reptiles / Sue Hamilton.
   p. cm. -- (Xtreme pets)
ISBN 978-1-61783-974-0
1. Reptiles--Juvenile literature. 2. Pets--Juvenile literature.   I. Title.
597.9--dc23

                                                              2013931676

CONTENTS

XTREME PETS: REPTILES

Reptile owners choose scales and claws over fur and paws. Reptiles make good pets, especially if the owner is allergic to furry animals. Some reptiles may be handled. With others, it is best to simply watch and be entertained.

A veiled chameleon eating a cricket.

XTREME FACT– A person who keeps pet reptiles is known as a "herpetoculturist."

SNAKES

nakes are a popular reptile pet. It is best to purchase captive-bred snakes as pets. Those taken from the wild may be sick. Also, wild snakes are an important part of an area's ecology and need to be left in their natural habitat.

Corn snakes are considered an excellent snake pet. They allow themselves to be gently handled. They are called "corn snakes" because they often live in areas where corn is grown. They prey on rodents that destroy crops. Corn snakes grow to be about 4-6 feet (1-2 m) in length. They are constrictors and eat live or frozen mice. Corn snakes live for about 15 to 20 years.

Corn Snake

Ball pythons are calm and gentle snakes. Also known as royal pythons, they make excellent pets. They live 15 to 20 years. They grow 3-4 feet (.9-1.2 m) in length. Ball pythons are active at night. They are constrictors. They kill by coiling around their prey and squeezing it. They eat mice and other small mammals and amphibians.

XTREME FACT– A ball python will curl up into a ball when frightened.

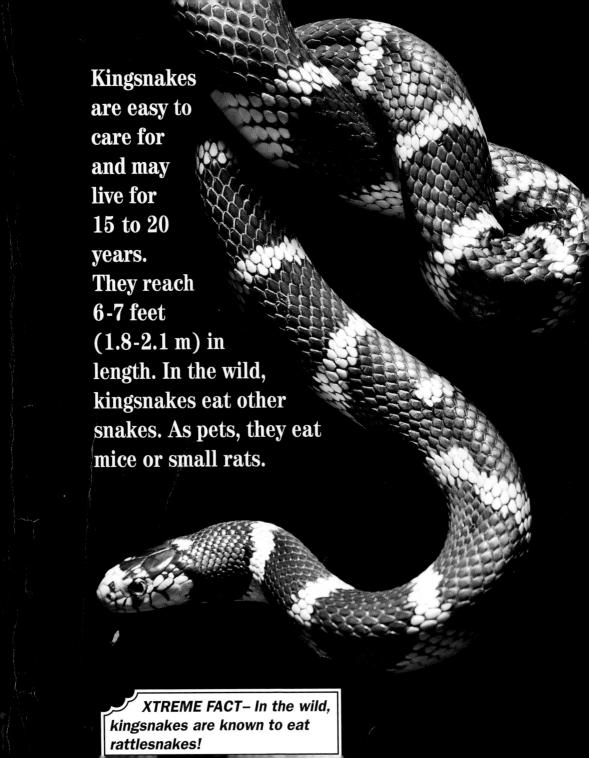

Kingsnakes are easy to care for and may live for 15 to 20 years. They reach 6-7 feet (1.8-2.1 m) in length. In the wild, kingsnakes eat other snakes. As pets, they eat mice or small rats.

XTREME FACT– In the wild, kingsnakes are known to eat rattlesnakes!

DRAGONS

Bearded dragons enjoy being carefully handled. While fierce looking, they are gentle pets that may live up to 10 years. The "beard" is a line of spines that stands up when they are threatened. Native to Australia, bearded dragons must be kept warm. They typically live in an aquarium tank with a few rocks or logs. They like to perch just off the ground.

Bearded Dragon

Beardies are omnivores. They eat insects, such as crickets and superworms, as well as green vegetables. They grow to about 24 inches (61 cm) in length.

XTREME FACT – Bearded dragons may run on their hind legs to escape danger.

Chinese water dragons are native to Asia. They grow bigger than their Australian cousins, reaching up to 36 inches (91 cm) in length. As their name implies, they are water dwellers. They need enclosures that allow them to be in water up to at least half their height. The water must be cleaned daily. Water dragons live about 15 years. They eat crickets, minnows, mice, green leafy vegetables, and some fruits.

Chinese
Water Dragon

XTREME FACT– Chinese water dragons whip their long tails at threatening predators.

MONITORS

Savannah monitors are not for beginning reptile pet owners. Savannahs must be handled a lot as babies to become used to humans. They reach 3 to 4 feet (.9-1.2 m) in length and have a hard bite and long claws.

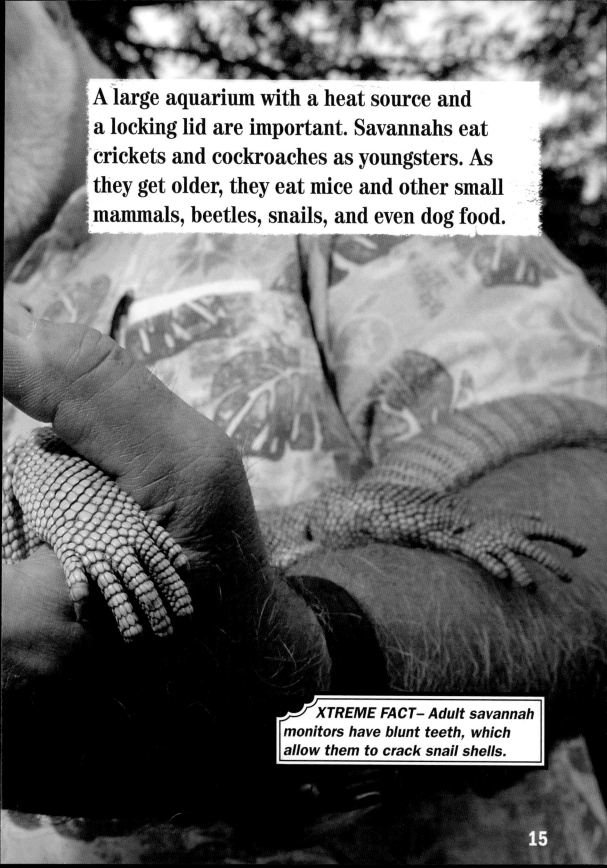

A large aquarium with a heat source and a locking lid are important. Savannahs eat crickets and cockroaches as youngsters. As they get older, they eat mice and other small mammals, beetles, snails, and even dog food.

XTREME FACT– Adult savannah monitors have blunt teeth, which allow them to crack snail shells.

IGUANAS

Iguanas are fascinating reptiles. They can grow to be very big. They may weigh up to 18 pounds (8 kg) and reach 4 to 6 feet (1-2 m) in length. Iguanas have strong, powerful jaws and razor-sharp teeth. They must be handled as babies to make good pets.

Iguanas need a lot of room and care. While babies may live in large aquariums, many owners have a room specifically for their adult iguanas. These pets live about 15 to 20 years. They must be kept warm and have plenty of water. Iguanas eat vegetables and fruits.

XTREME FACT – Iguanas are good swimmers. They propel themselves through water by moving their strong tails from side to side.

GECKOS

Geckos are small, easy-going pets. There are as many as 2,000 species of geckos. They need a warm, humid environment and a steady supply of water. Adults grow to a length of 8-10 inches (20-25 cm). They eat mealworms and crickets. A leopard gecko may live 15 to 20 years.

XTREME FACT– Most geckos cannot blink. They have fixed, transparent eyelids over their eyes. They clean them using their tongues! Their eyesight is 350 times more sensitive than a human's eyesight.

Leopard Gecko

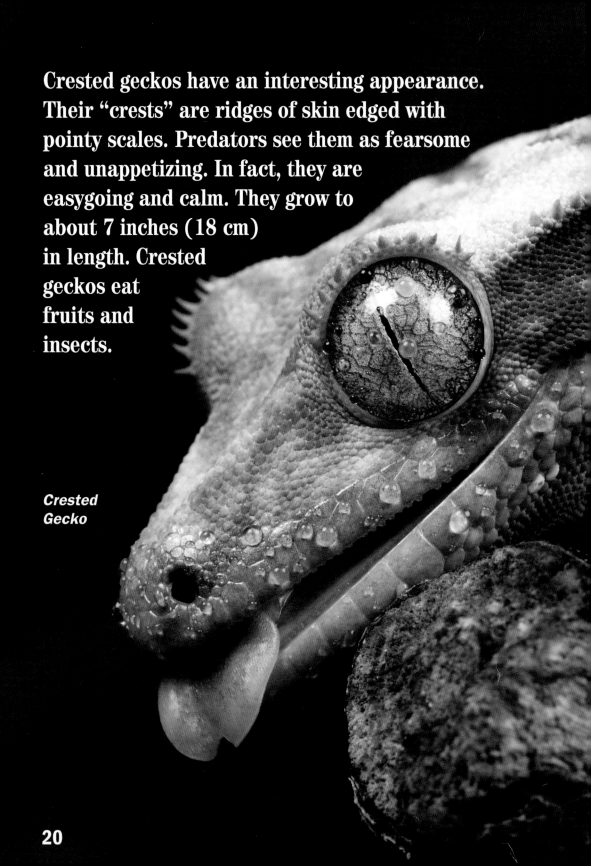

Crested geckos have an interesting appearance. Their "crests" are ridges of skin edged with pointy scales. Predators see them as fearsome and unappetizing. In fact, they are easygoing and calm. They grow to about 7 inches (18 cm) in length. Crested geckos eat fruits and insects.

Crested Gecko

XTREME FACT – Crested geckos were thought to be extinct in the 1900s. In 1994, they were rediscovered. Captive breeders helped increase their numbers. Crested geckos were offered for sale as pets again in 2002.

ANOLES

Green anoles are often called American chameleons, although they are not chameleons. They are small, growing to about 7 inches (18 cm) in length. They are very fragile creatures and should only be held when absolutely necessary.

XTREME FACT – *It only takes about a minute for a green anole to change color.*

These small lizards are fun to wa...
color. When they are cool or sleepy, ...
brown. When they are warm or active, the...
green. Anoles love to run, climb, and jump. They
need a large vertical enclosure with plenty of
sunshine. Anoles eat insects such as crickets
and mealworms. They usually live for 3 to 5
years, but may live up to 10 years.

Anole

CHAMELEONS

Chameleons have unusual qualities that make them fun pets. They have eyes that move independent of each other. They can change color to blend in with their surroundings. Their super-long, sticky-tipped tongues dart out to catch insects, spiders, millipedes, and small lizards. There are about 160 different species of chameleons. They grow to about 2 feet (.6 m) in length. They live for 5 to 10 years.

A chameleon about to eat a grasshopper.

XTREME FACT– A chameleon's tongue is about 1½ times its body length. If a 6-foot-tall (2-m) human had that feature, that person would have a 9-foot-long (3-m) tongue!

SKINKS

Skinks are slow-moving, ground-dwelling lizards. They are fairly gentle and may live 10 to 20 years. There are more than 1,200 species of skinks.

XTREME FACT – When threatened, a skink stops, opens its mouth, hisses, and flattens its body to look bigger. At this point, if the threat gets closer, it will bite–and often not let go!

Blue-tongued skinks are common skink pets. They grow to be about 18 inches (46 cm) long. Just as their name implies, they have a blue tongue inside a bright pink mouth. The blue tongue frightens off predators. Skinks eat fruits and vegetables, as well as mice and worms.

TURTLES & TORTOISES

If you want a pet that could outlive you, turtles and tortoises are for you. Some live for 40 to 100 years! These pets can get very big, and need special care. Turtles spend most of their lives in the water. The most popular pet turtles are red-eared sliders. They can grow to be 12 inches (30 cm) long. They need a large pond-like tank with a dry basking area. They eat packaged turtle food, as well as worms, crickets, and leafy greens.

XTREME FACT – Turtles and tortoises may carry certain types of bacteria, such as salmonella. It is important that anyone who touches or cares for these pets wash their hands thoroughly.

Tortoises spend most of their lives on land. They need a shallow water dish to drink from or soak in. Leopard tortoises are common pets. Average adults weigh 40 pounds (18 kg), but they can grow three times as big!

Tortoises graze on grasses, prickly pears, and thistles. They may also enjoy vegetables and an occasional piece of fruit.

GLOSSARY

AMPHIBIAN
A class of animals that includes frogs, newts, toads, and salamanders.

CAPTIVE-BRED
A creature that is not born in the wild. Captive-bred reptile pets are usually healthier and more likely to take to living with humans.

CONSTRICTORS
Snakes who kill prey by surrounding them with their muscular bodies and squeezing so the prey cannot breathe.

ECOLOGY

The balanced relationship between a specific environment and the creatures that live there. If, for example, all corn snakes were taken away from an area, the area would likely be overrun with mice.

FRAGILE

Easily broken or hurt.

HABITAT

The natural home of a living thing. When owners recreate their pets's natural habitats, the animals live healthier, longer, and happier lives.

MAMMALS

Warm-blooded animals with hair or fur that give birth to live young.

OMNIVORES

Creatures that eat both plants and animals as food.

PREDATORS

An animal that preys on other animals.

RODENTS

A group of small animals with teeth that gnaw, including mice, rats, gerbils, hamsters, squirrels, and porcupines. This is the largest group of mammals.

INDEX

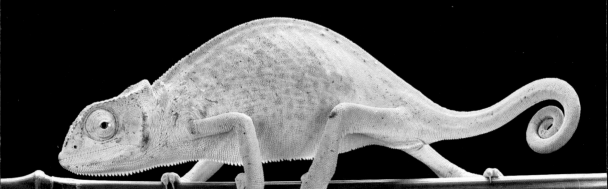